Especially for Primary

Class Symbols and the Primary Theme in Counted Cross Stitch

Designed by

Jean D. Crowther

Acknowledgments

Grateful appreciation is extended to all who worked with care to produce this book:

- The editorial and technical staff of Horizon Publishers,
- Shane and Sharon Burnham, the chart drafters,
- Tracy Price, Renae Hale and Sharon Burnham, the model stitchers.
- *Winchelt Imports* (Stoddard, WI), for the fabric for the model of the Theme and "My Heavenly Father Loves Me." (#355101 Antique White 16-count Aida Cloth),
- *The DMC Corporation* (Elizabeth, NJ) and *J. & P. Coats* (Jacksonville, FL), for the floss for the models,
- *Maderia USA Ltd.* (Laconia, NH) for the metalized thread,
- *Apple Frame Gallery* (Bountiful, UT) and *Wheatland Crafts, Inc.* (Simpsonville, SC) for the frames.

Appreciation is also expressed to the LDS Church Copyrights and Permissions Office, the General Primary Presidency, and Janice Piccolo of the Primary General board for their counsel and permission to use copyrighted materials,

And gratitude is expressed to Standard Publishing Company for permission to use the copyrighted drawing of Frances Hook, and its licensing of the drawing's cross stitch design to Horizon Publishers.

I hope that many will enjoy the opportunity to stitch these designs for themselves and for the Primary children, and to share them with family and friends. May they be a source of strength and inspiration.

Jean D. Crowther

First Printing, March 1990

Printing: 1 2 3 4 5 6 7 8 9 10

International Standard Book Number
0-88290-391-8

Horizon Publishers' Catalog and Order Number
2772

Horizon Publishers
& Distributors, Incorporated
P.O. Box 490 Bountiful, Utah 84011-0490

DMC®

TABLE OF CONTENTS

INTRODUCTION

The Primary organization is an auxiliary of The Church of Jesus Christ of Latter-day Saints for children ages 3-11. The purpose of Primary is to teach the children the gospel of Jesus Christ and help them learn to live it. It exists to help the children grow in the knowledge and love of Heavenly Father and Jesus Christ, to prepare them for baptism, to keep their baptismal covenants and to gain an understanding of the gospel plan. The girls are taught to prepare to fulfill their roles as righteous young women and to live lives of service. The boys are taught to prepare to receive the priesthood and to be worthy to use it to bless the lives of others.

There are six basic class groups in the Primary. Each has a class symbol, the oldest four also have class mottos. There are also two statements of declaration and a lovely drawing of Jesus interacting with young children that seemed appropriate to use in this book.

The book has been developed to reinforce that which is taught in Primary. Each chart has been carefully designed to help the children and their leaders

1. create a beautiful reminder of the theme, class symbols and statements for their personal use,
2. follow the original designs and colors, as designated by the Primary leaders, as faithfully as possible within the limits set by even-weave materials,
3. have simple patterns that will allow even the beginner to stitch quickly and be satisfied with the work. The class symbols are designed as solid pieces. However, they may be stitched more simply by working only the backstitch outline without filling in the solid-color stitching.

INSTRUCTIONS

Basic Cross Stitch—Form a habit of always cross stitching in the same direction for a uniform appearance. If the bottom diagonal slants from the lower left hole to the upper right, all bottom diagonals should be in that same direction (see Figure 1). Use a hoop to keep the stitches uniform in tension.

Half Stitch—In some areas, the graph will show a smaller symbol in one corner of a square. To create this half stitch, work from the corner hole into the center of the square, placing the needle between the threads (see Figure 2). Complete the stitch with either a full diagonal across the other angle or the backstitch outline color where designated.

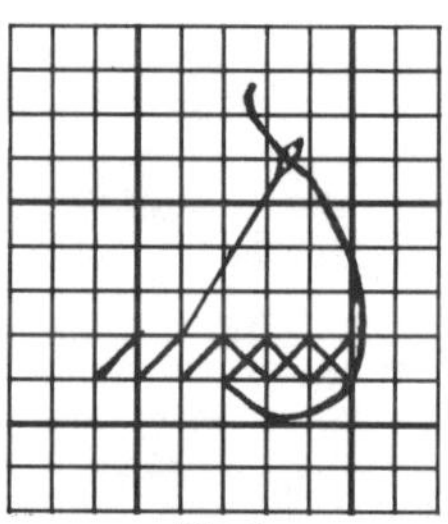
Fig. 1

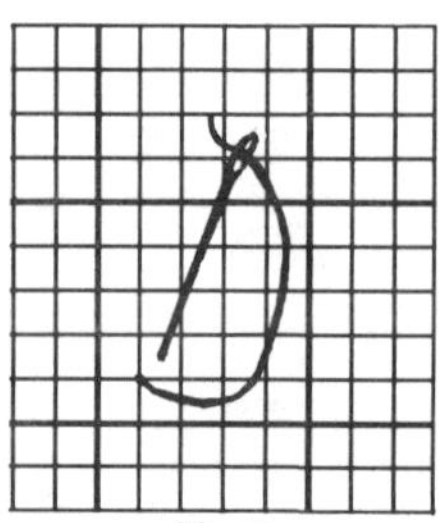
Fig. 2

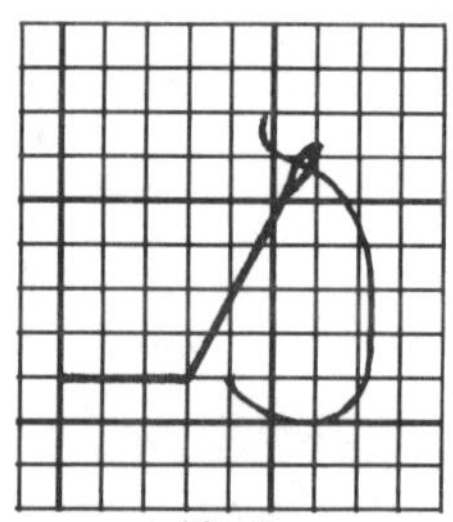
Fig. 3

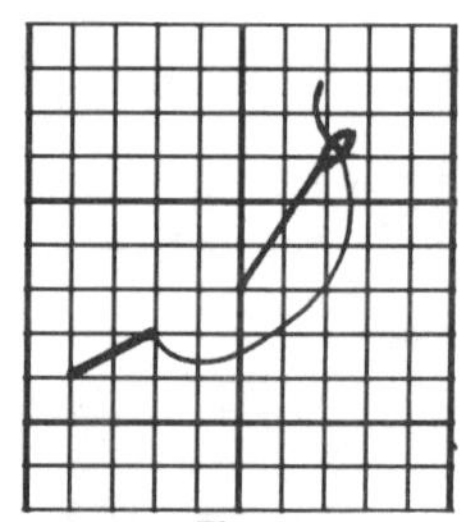
Fig. 4

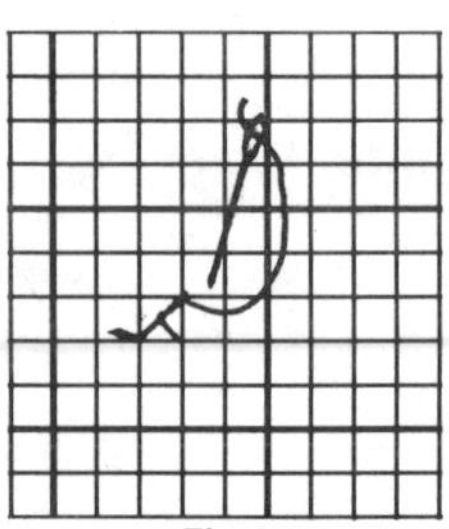
Fig. 5

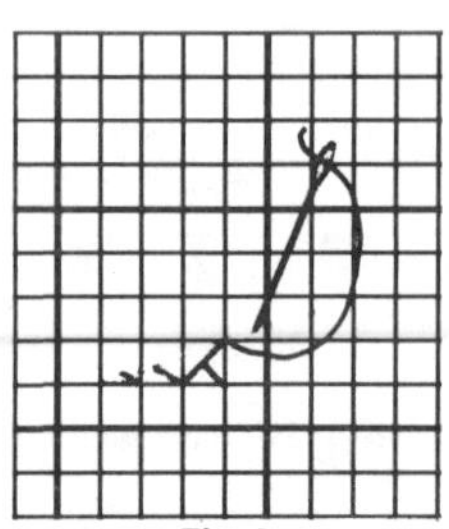
Fig. 6

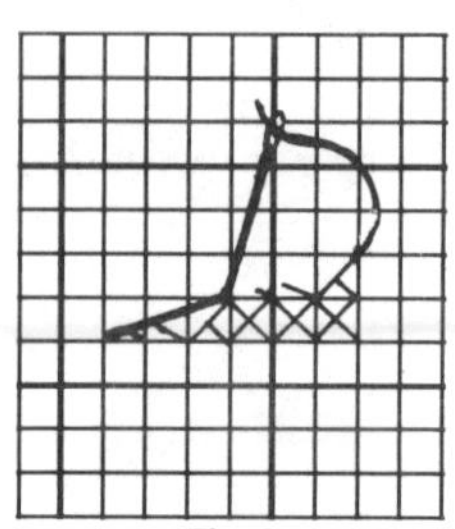
Fig. 7

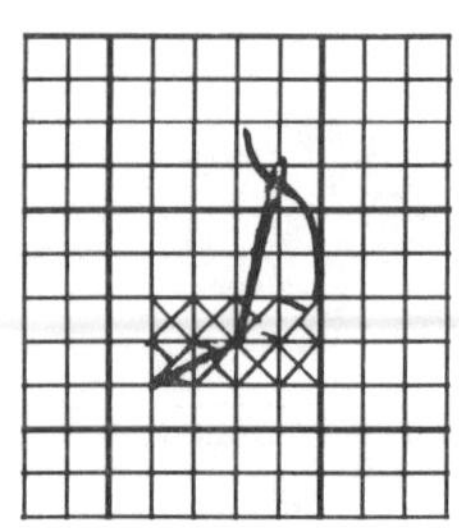
Fig. 8

Backstitch Outline—Anchor the thread and bring the needle up in an appropriate place in the pattern. Place the needle down in the hole behind the initial stitch. Continue working one stitch length back on top of the fabric and two stitches forward beneath the fabric to form a solid line (see Figure 3).

"Over-two" and "Over-three" Backstitch—To create a gentler line, two stitches have been created. The terms "over-two" and "over-three" refer to the distance a single backstitch will travel over the squares vertically or horizontally (see Figure 4). Care must be taken with these longer stitches to keep the tension even.

When working cross stitches to fill in the squares of the areas created by "over-two" or "over-three" backstitches, it is necessary to make a different-angled stitch. A true half stitch will not work.

To fill in the colors next to an "over-two" backstitch, begin at the corner hole of the narrowest square and make a very shallow-angled half stitch. The adjoining square can be filled in with a standard half stitch (see Figure 5). The "over-three" fill-in will be done in the same manner, increasing the first two angles (see Figures 6 and 7). When two different colors meet it is necessary to use the same fill-in techniques for both colors (see Figure 8). Sometimes it's easier to backstitch first and then carefully fill in the cross stitches, making sure to stay inside the backstitches as your needle enters the material.

Material Needed—The design size is given on each page. To calculate the finished size of your design in inches, divide the count of your material into each number. Add at least two inches to each of the four sides of the design size to allow adequate material for finishing or framing.

Floss Needed—The general rule is to use one less strand for backstitching than was used for cross stitching. However, more strands may be added to create the distinct lines of the lettering and the backstitch-outlined symbols. The stitcher should experiment in order to achieve the desired effect. When using extra strands of floss, care must be taken to keep the tension even. Suggested amounts are:

Material Count	*Cross-Stitches*	*Backstitching*
11-count Aida	3 strands	2-4 strands
14- or 16-count Aida	2 strands	1-3 strands
18-count Aida	1-2 strands	1-2 strands
Linen worked over 2 squares	1-2 strands	1-2 strands
22-count Hardanger	1-2 strands	1-2 strands

The color numbers are given for three major brands of floss generally available. Listings are given for embroidery floss from *The DMC Corporation of Elizabeth, NJ; Anchor* made by Susan Bates of Chester, CT, and *Wound Embroidery Floss* manufactured by J. & P. Coats of Jacksonville, FL. Because of individual color-matching differences, floss from the different companies should not be mixed in a single stitchery design.

Finishing Instructions—Always stitch with clean hands. Even if your completed stitchery doesn't appear soiled, it is still best to hand-wash it with mild soap and warm water when finished, just as you would fine lingerie. Rinse carefully and blot with a clean bath towel without wringing, folding, or squeezing the material. Place the wet stitchery, floss-side down, on a dry bath towel, making sure the fabric isn't twisted. Iron with a hot iron until completely dry and the background cloth looks smooth. Use a pressing cloth if metallic thread has been used. Handle it carefully until it's permanently mounted.

PRIMARY THEME

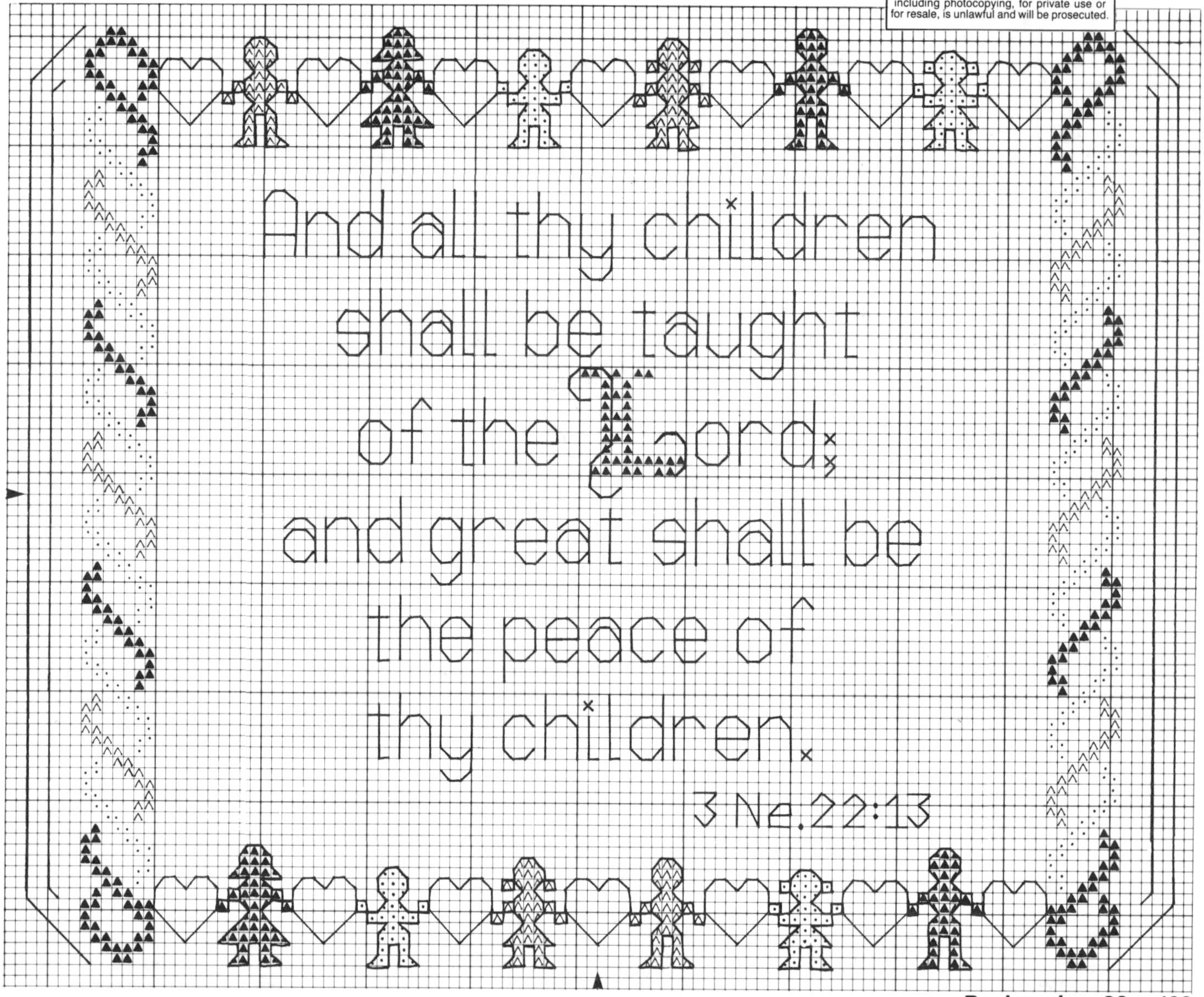

Design size: 86 x 108

Symbol	DMC	Anchor	JPCoats	Color Name	Object
Λ	321	47	3500	red	medium children & chain
•	973	290	2290	yellow	small children & chain
▲	797	132	7023	blue	large chilren, L & chain
———	3371	382	5381	black-brown	lettering
▬▬▬				gold	metallic thread in L*
———	321	47	3500	red	outline hearts*
———	797	132	7023	blue	4 vertical side lines*

Special Stitching Instructions

* Two strands of a metallic thread, such as *Maderia's* Article #9842, style #40 (color gold-4), is suggested for the highlighting of the capital L. Also mix two strands of gold thread in the needle with the red and blue floss to accent the hearts and vertical side lines.

Backstitch outline the blue and red children with one strand of the color in which they are stitched. Use blue floss to outline the yellow children so they will show up.

I AM A CHILD OF GOD

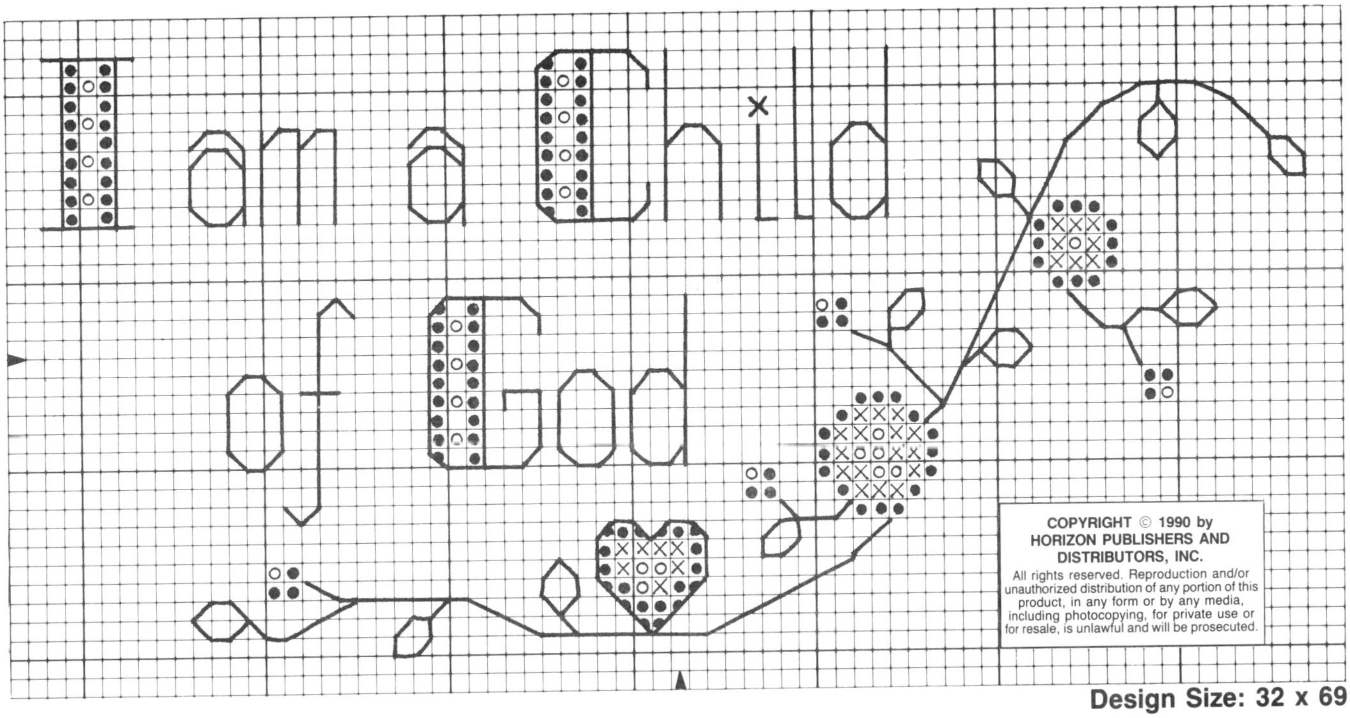

Design Size: 32 x 69

This design can be worked in any combination of a dark and light shade plus an accent color and a green for the vine and leaves. Colors used in the model are:

Symbol	DMC	Anchor	JPCoats	Color Name	Object
X	932	920	7050	light blue	flowers, inside letters
●	930	922	7052	dark blue	flowers
○	745	300	2292	light yellow	flowers, inside letters
———	930	922	7052	dark blue	lettering
———	986	245	6258	dark green	vines and leaf lines

Special Stitching Instructions

One strand of a gold blending filament or metallic thread such as *Maderia's* Article #9842, style #40 (color gold-4) can be combined in the needle with the floss to enhance the design.

This chart can be finished in a variety of ways. It has been specifically designed to fit the **Quilted Cloth CarryAll™**, with an Aida-cloth pocket, manufactured by Horizon Publishers and Distributors, Inc. (Bountiful, UT). The **CarryAll™** will hold both the standard size *Bible* and *Triple Combination.* It is available in slate blue (style #3891X) and in colonial pink (style #3890X). The colors listed above will match the blue quilted cloth. The pink cloth matches the DMC colors #961-963. If the **CarryAll™** is not stocked by your local LDS bookstore you may obtain ordering information and prices by writing to Horizon Publishers.

The **CarryAll™** may be personalized by stitching the name or monogram in the bottom right corner.

JESUS AND THE CHILDREN

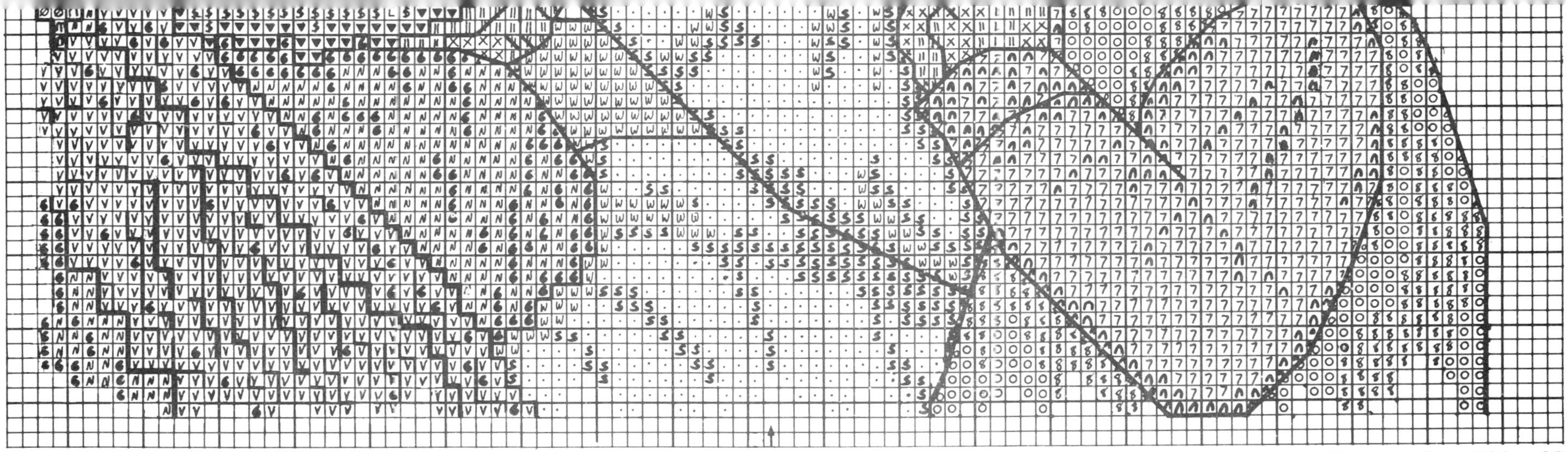

Artwork by Frances Hook. © 1962. S. P. Co.

Design size: 111 x 98

Object	Symbol	DMC	Color Description
Jesus' Hair & Beard	L	729	medium gold
	8	434	dark gold brown
	◢	801	chocolate brown
	——	801	chocolate brown—*backstitch hair*
Jesus' Flesh & Hands	—	951	light olive flesh
	c	945	medium olive flesh
	3	950	dark olive flesh
	I	353	light salmon
	■	801	chocolate brown—*eye*
	——	632	flesh outline—*backstitch*
Jesus' Robe	•	746	light cream
	w	3046	medium cream
	s	3047	dark cream
	L	729	medium gold
	(daisy stitch) *	729	medium gold—*daisy stitch design*
	——	780	deep gold brown—*backstitch robe*
Children's Flesh	+	712	light flesh
	×	948	medium flesh
	II	754	dark flesh
	I	353	light salmon
	ε	352	salmon
	□	blanc neige	white
	——	632	flesh outline—*backstitch*

Object	Symbol	DMC	Color Description
Left Girl's Hair & Eye	L	729**	medium gold
	z	301	copper
	◤	300	dark copper
	——	300	dark copper—*backstitch hair*
	■	517	dark aqua blue—*eye*
Left Girl's Clothes	ø	518	medium aqua blue
	n	743	medium yellow
	——	517	dark aqua blue—*backstitch sash*
Back Boy's Hair & Eyes	▿	437	tan
	●	435	medium gold brown
	——	435	medium gold brown—*backstitch hair*
	■	801	chocolate brown—*eyes*
Back Boy's Clothes	y	554	lilac
	ʌ	553	light violet
	——	553	light violet—*backstitch robe*
	(flower) *	743	medium yellow—*flower*
	——	3348	medium green—*flower stem*

Object	Symbol	DMC	Color Description
Front Boy's Hair	L	729	medium gold
	$	780	deep gold brown
	▾	839	dark brown
	——	839	dark brown—*backstitch hair*
Front Boy's Clothes	N	519	light aqua blue
	6	517	dark aqua blue
	v	3348	medium green
	——	517	dark aqua blue—*backstitch robe*
	——***	498	scarlet—*backstitch robe*
Right Girl's Hair & Eye	7	745	light yellow
	=	744	lemon yellow
	▿	437	tan
	——	435	medium gold brown—*backstitch hair*
	■	517	dark aqua blue—*eye*
Right Girl's Clothes	7	745	light yellow
	n	743	medium yellow
	ʌ	553	light violet
	o	436	light gold brown
	8	434	dark gold brown
	——	434	dark gold brown—*backstitch clothes*

Special stitching instructions

* Work the areas behind the two sets of lazy daisy stitches in the colors indicated in surrounding squares (Jesus' robe in #3047, back boy's robe in #554). Then work the lazy daisy stitch on top in the colors indicated. A small dot is given in the design to mark the exact placement of both ends of the stitch. Follow the backstitch outline on Jesus' robe to connect the daisy stitches.

If an auburn hair color is desired, use one strand each of two colors of floss, DMC #729 and #349, in the needle for the **L symbol instead of two strands of #729.

The eyes of each figure are worked with solid colors as indicated. A small half stitch of white highlight is then added on top of the solid color.

Be sure to read the instructions on page 5 for directions on how to stitch and fill in the over-two and over-three backstitches.

It will prove easiest to complete one figure at a time in this project, beginning with the back boy and working forward. Be careful to use the proper backstitch color. If in doubt, decide which figure is in the front and use that proper color.

SUNBEAM CLASS SYMBOL

Design size: 73 x 54

Symbol	DMC	Anchor	JPCoats	Color Name	Object
•	973	290	2290	yellow	sun inside
/	741	314	2319	orange	sun points
———	349	13	2335	red-orange	sun outline
———	3371	382	5381	black-brown	lettering

Special Stitching Instructions

Be sure to read the instructions on page 5 for directions on how to stitch and fill in the over-two and over-three backstitches.

STAR CLASS SYMBOL

Design size: 76 x 57

Symbol	DMC	Anchor	JPCoats	Color Name	Object
•	973	290	2290	yellow	star inside
———	3371	382	5381	black-brown	star outline and lettering

Special Stitching Instructions

Be sure to read the instructions on page 5 for directions on how to stitch and fill in the over-two and over-three backstitches.

CTR CLASS SYMBOL AND MOTTO

Alternate Line

The first line of the motto may be changed from "I can" to "I will" to indicate a stronger commitment. Center the alternate line carefully.

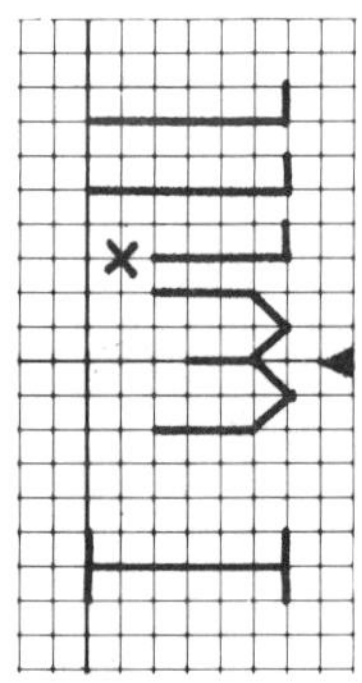

Design size: 78 x 57

Symbol	DMC	Anchor	JPCoats	Color Name	Object
ǀǀ	699	229	6228	dark green	inside CTR and border
•	973	290	2290	yellow	background
——	3371	382	5381	black-brown	symbol outline and motto lettering

Special Stitching Instructions

Be sure to read the instructions on page 5 for directions on how to stitch and fill in the over-two and over-three backstitches.

VALIANT CLASS SYMBOL AND MOTTO

Alternate Line

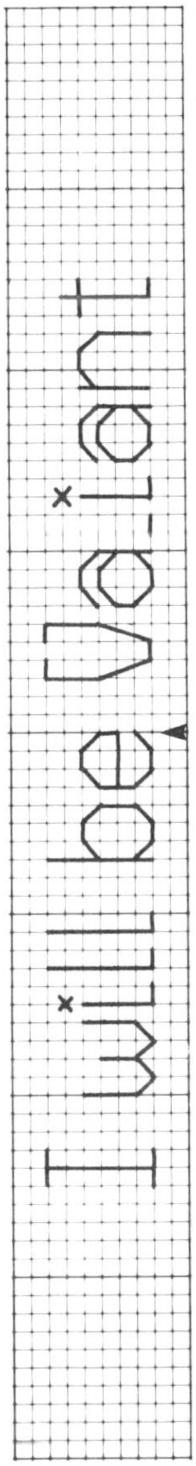

The first line of the motto may be changed from "I can" to "I will" to indicate a stronger commitment.
Center the alternate line carefully.

Design size:
91 x 70

Symbol	DMC	Anchor	JPCoats	Color Name	Object
open square	blanc neige	1	1001	white	child and man
3	970	314	2099	orange	middle banner
I	972	302	2303	light orange	internal borders
•	973	290	2290	yellow	background
▬ (heavy line)	666	46	3046	bright red	VALIANT letters
——	349	13	3019	red-orange	symbol outline
——	3371	382	5381	black-brown	motto lettering

Special Stitching Instructions

Be sure to read the instructions on page 5 for directions on how to stitch and fill in the over-two and over-three backstitches. This design is one that might prove easier to backstitch the basic outlines first and then fill in.

MERRIE MISS CLASS SYMBOL AND MOTTO

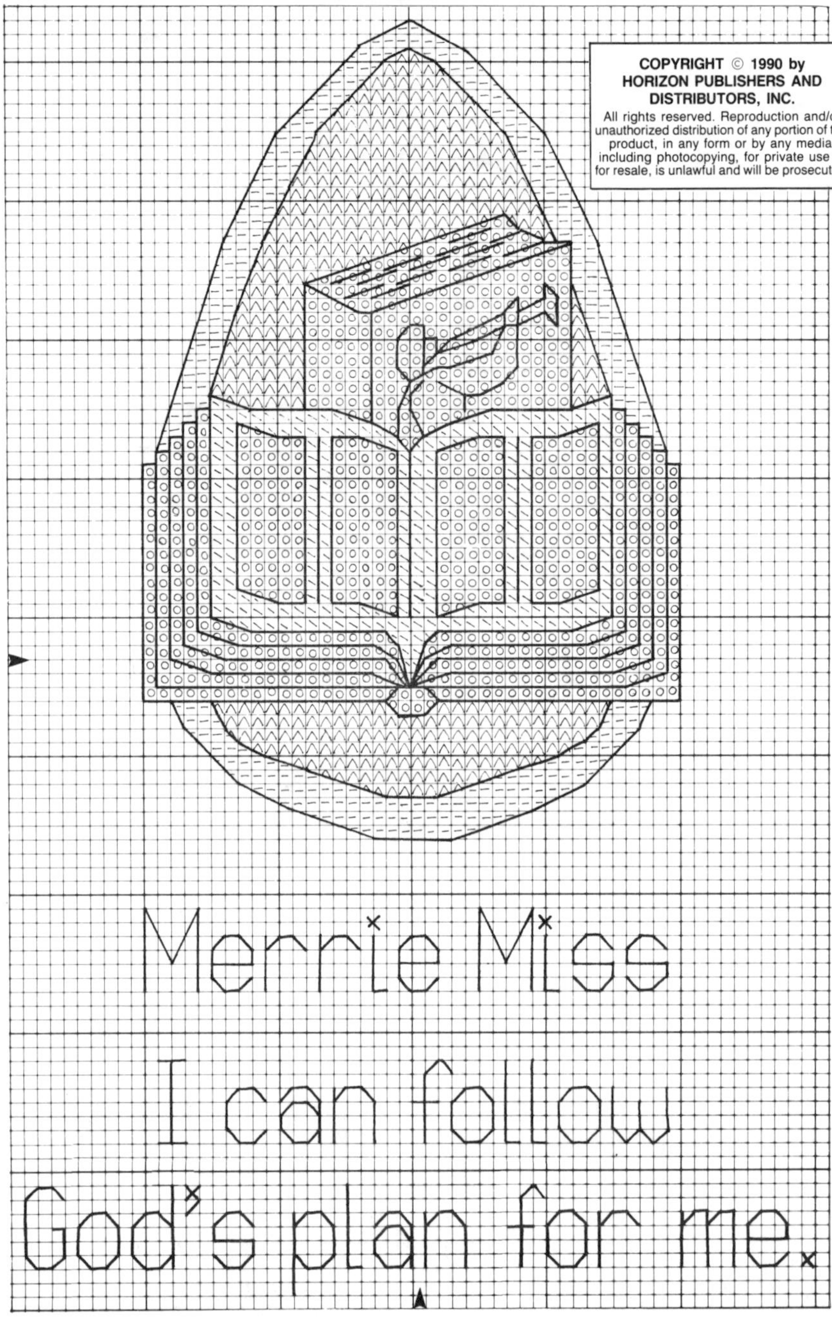

Alternate Line

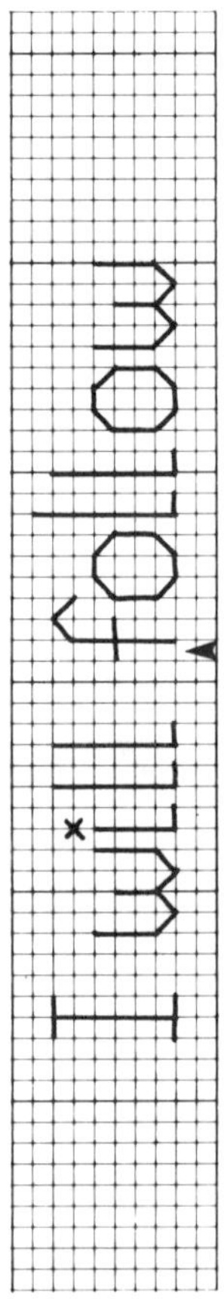

The first line of the motto may be changed from "I can" to "I will" to indicate a stronger commitment. Center the alternate line carefully.

Design size: 93 x 59

Symbol	DMC	Anchor	JPCoats	Color Name	Object
O	725	297	2298	gold	book cover, edges, columns
\	745	300	2292	light yellow	book page borders
—	3326	24	3126	light salmon	symbol border
Λ	321	47	3500	dark salmon	background
———	434	309	5000	brown	book and pages outline
———	3371	382	5381	black-brown	symbol outline and motto lettering

Special Stitching Instructions

Be sure to read the instructions on page 5 for directions on how to stitch and fill in the over-two and over-three backstitches.

BLAZER CLASS SYMBOL AND MOTTO

Alternate Line

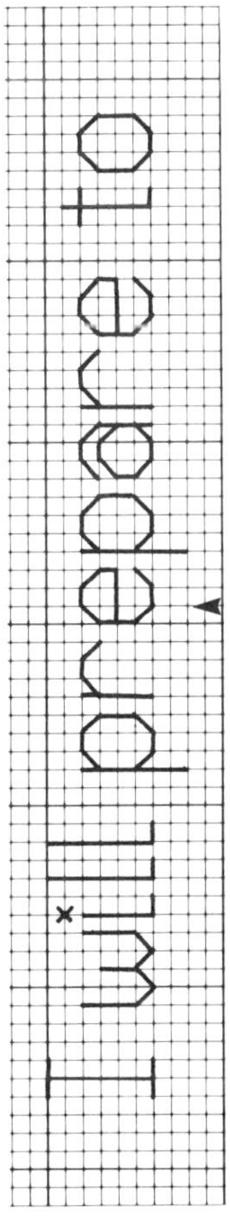

The first line of the motto may be changed from "I can" to "I will" to indicate a stronger commitment. Center the alternate line carefully.

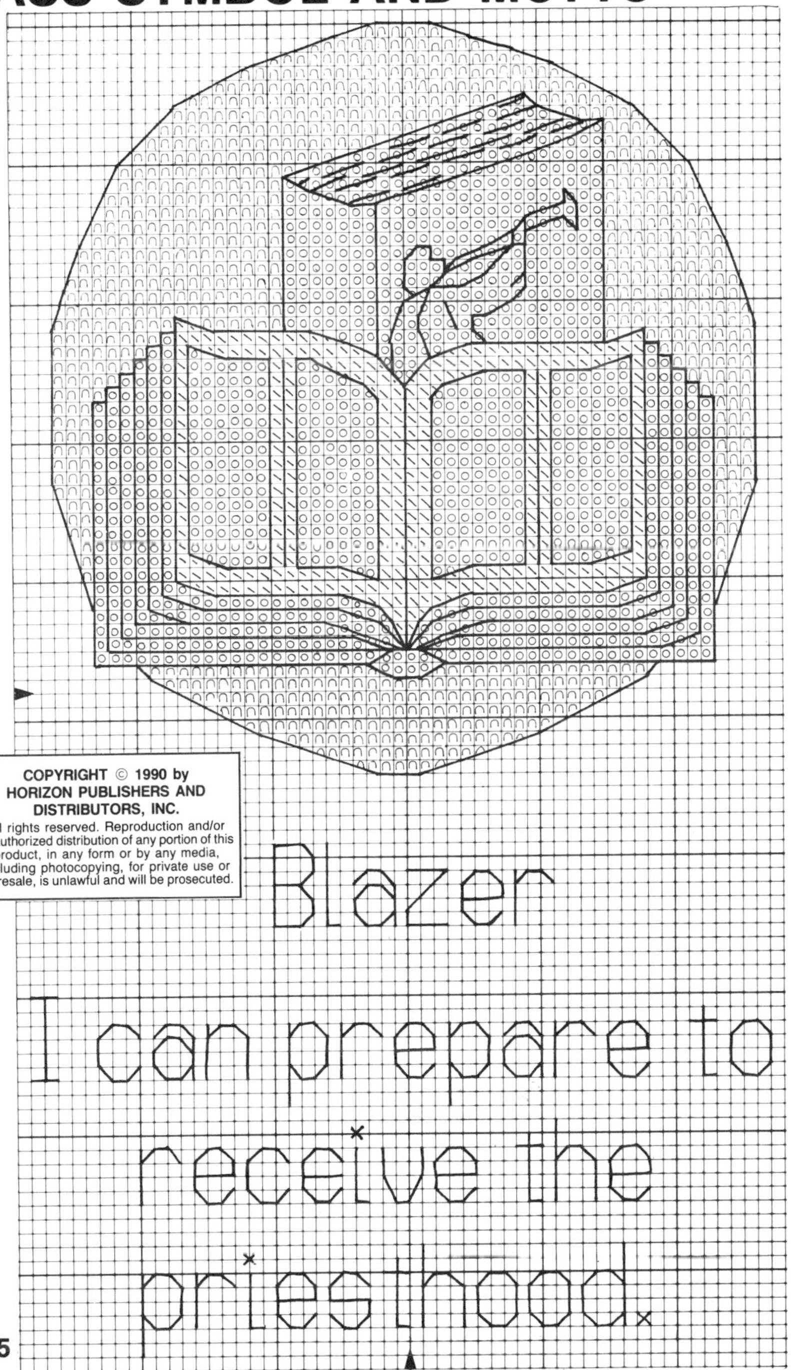

Design size: 96 x 55

Symbol	DMC	Anchor	JPCoats	Color Name	Object
	725	297	2298	gold	book cover, edges, columns
o	745	300	2292	light yellow	book page borders
∩	718	87	3088	plum	background
———	434	309	5000	brown	book and pages outline
———	915	89	3090	dark plum	symbol circle outline
———	3371	382	5381	black-brown	motto lettering

Special Stitching Instructions

Be sure to read the instructions on page 5 for directions on how to stitch and fill in the over-two and over-three backstitches.

MY HEAVENLY FATHER LOVES ME

Design size: 88 x 92

This design can be stitched in any combination of three colors. The model is stitched in the following:

Symbol	DMC	Anchor	JPCoats	Color Name	Object
◣	309	29	3401	dark rose	heart border
▬ (thick line)	930	922	7052	slate blue	lettering*
— (thin line)	76	25	3281	pink	background around heart*

Special Stitching Instructions

*The words "Heavenly Father" have two strands of an iridescent blending filament added to the two strands of slate blue in the needle for emphasis. The background is stitched with one strand of pink and two strands of the iridescent blending filament. *Maderia's* Article #9850, No. 50, (Color 4C4) was used.

It is suggested that a frame for this design be chosen before beginning the project and the background be extended to cover all the visible Aida cloth between the heart border and the frame edge. The model is stitched on 16 count Aida cloth and mounted diagonally in a *Wheatland Crafts, Inc.* Oak Thinline frame (#TL5x5).